Collard J. Stock

Translations in Verse

from the French, Spanish, Portuguese, Italian, Swedish, German and Dutch

Collard J. Stock

Translations in Verse
from the French, Spanish, Portuguese, Italian, Swedish, German and Dutch

ISBN/EAN: 9783337231095

Printed in Europe, USA, Canada, Australia, Japan

Cover: Foto ©Andreas Hilbeck / pixelio.de

More available books at **www.hansebooks.com**

Translations in Verse

FROM THE

French, Spanish, Portuguese, Italian, Swedish, German, and Dutch.

BY

COLLARD J. STOCK.

LONDON:

ELLIOT STOCK, 62, PATERNOSTER ROW, E.C.

1891.

ARISE · PRAY · WORK

CONTENTS.

FROM THE FRENCH.

FROM THE SPANISH.

FROM THE PORTUGUESE.

FROM THE ITALIAN.

FROM THE SWEDISH.

FROM THE GERMAN.

FROM THE DUTCH.

FROM THE FRENCH

A

SONNET.

FROM THE FRENCH OF FÉLIX ARVERS.

M Y soul its secret hath, my life its mystery ;
    A love eternal at a breath conceived :
The ill is hopeless—silent I have lived,
And she that wrought it ne'er has known of me.
I shall pass near her—ah ! she will not see ;
Still at her side yet lonely I must wend,
And serve my time on earth until the end,
Not daring aught to ask, unguerdoned be.
And she, whom God so tender made and sweet,
Will go her way, absorbed, and will not-hear
This murmur of my love that tracks her feet ;
But, faithful to her duty, calm, austere,
Will say, if e'er these lines her eyes should greet,
' Who is this woman ?' ever unaware !

THE BENEDICTION.

FROM THE FRENCH OF FRANÇOIS COPPÉE.

WE took Saragossa in the year eighteen-nine.
    I was sergeant : a terrible day's work was
mine.
The town was captured—the houses by storm we
    took
That still closely shut up had a treacherous look.
From their windows the shots in showers came rain-
    ing :
' 'Tis the fault of the priests' the men muttered, com-
    plaining ;
So that when in the distance we saw them in flight,
Although hard we had fought from the first dawning
    light,
With our eyes by dust blinded, mouths bitter and
    black
From the cartridge's sombre kiss 'midst the smoke's
    rack,

4

We fired gaily and always more briskly disposed
At all those long dark cloaks and broad hats dis-
    closed.
My battalion followed a deep narrow lane ;
I marched watching the roofs right and left, not in
    vain,
In my rank as sergeant with the light infantry.
Then I saw a swift, sudden red glare in the
    sky,
That faded and glowed like a forge's hot breath ;
We heard loud shrieks of women butchered to death
Afar off, 'midst the hoarse and funereal din.
We strode o'er the dead at each moment ; within
Dark hovels our men entered, lowering the head,
Then came out with their bayonets reeking and
    red,
And with the blood on their hands marked a cross on
    the wall ;
For in these narrow passes we made sure before all
That behind us we had not left one of our foes.
We advanced without drum-beat, no war-march
    arose,
And thoughtful our officers looked ; the veterans,
    too,
Were anxious, keeping shoulder to shoulder all
    through,

For, as if we were mere raw recruits, our hearts
    sank.

All at once, at the turn of a street deep and dank,

Shouts for help from French voices were heard : rush-
    ing on

We reached our friends in peril and straight fell upon

A troop of gallant grenadiers in full retreat,

Driven ingloriously out into the street

From a convent's enclosure, only defended

By a score of swart monks, who like demons de-
    scended

With shaven crowns and black robes with white cross
    woven :

Barefoot, with blood-stained arms, their sleeves all
    cloven,

They struck our men down, each with a crucifix im-
    mense.

It was tragic.   We opened a platoon fire dense,

I and the others there, and so swept clear the place.

Coldly, cruelly—for the troops, worn out, felt base

And butcherlike dealing around this hangman's fate—

We killed that dreadful group of heroes at the gate :

But when once consummated was this vile deed of
    war,

And when the thick gray smoke had blown on high
    afar,

6

We saw beneath the bodies that entangled lay
Long rivulets of blood run down the steps away.
Behind, with open door, the gloomy church loomed
    vast.
The lights, like stars of gold, through dusk their
    radiance cast,
The incense all around its languorous perfume shed,
And deep in the choir tow'rds the altar turned his
    head,
As though no sound of battle had reached his ear at all,
A white-haired priest whose figure towered grave and
    tall :
The office of the day he was ending tranquilly.
This evil memory comes back so clear to me,
That while I tell you now I seem to see again
The old convent with its high Moorish-fronted fane,
The dead monks' great brown bodies, the hot sun that
    shone,
Making the crimson blood smoke on the pavement
    stone,
And through the black frame of the low door's dark
    outline
That priest and that altar glittering like a shrine,
And ourselves standing, fixed there, looking almost
    cowed.
At that time of my life I was one who swore loud,

A godless young fellow, and still many can tell
How once, when our troopers were sacking a
  chapel,
Just to show off my pluck and my wit, I would
  dare
Light my pipe at the high altar candles, nor care
What I did—hard campaigner—in impudence sheer—
But so white looked that old man he filled me with
  fear.

' Fire !' cried an officer.

                      No one moved.   The priest heard
For certain, but of that not a sign once appeared,
And he faced us, with the sacrament in his hand ;
For the mass now had reached the point, you under-
  stand,
Where the priest turns to bless the faithful.   O'er the
  head
His arms raised high aloft almost like wings seemed
  spread,
And each one backward shrank when with the gold
  monstrance
He made the sign of the cross in the air.   His glance
Told that he no more feared than before flock devout ;
And when his fine voice, chanting and lengthening
  out

The notes, as the priests all do in their *Oremus*,
Said

> '*Benedicat vos omnipotens Deus*,'

'Fire !' cried again the fierce voice, 'or you reckon
    with me.'
Then one of our men, a soldier—a coward was he—
At last levelled his musket and fired.   The old man
Turned very pale, but fearless once more began,
Not lowering his gaze, flashing with courage stern ;
'*Pater et Filius*,' he said.

>   What rage could turn
Or what bloodthirsty madness overwhelm man's brain
Enough to send a shot then from our ranks again ?
I know not ; and yet that infamous deed was done.
The monk, with one hand grasping the altar, still
    held on,
And trying once more to bless us—it must be told—
Raised with the other hand the great monstrance of
    gold.
For the third time he traced the sign of pardon :
    now,
With a voice that sounded far away and faint and low,
But well we heard it, for deep silence came on us,
He said, with closing eyes,

>   '*Et Spiritus Sanctus*,'

9

Then fell dead, having ended his last prayer.
The monstrance thrice rebounded on the stone, and
    there
Even we, the old troopers, were standing hushed,
    aghast,
Gazing with gloomy eyes as we grounded arms at
    last,
With horror in our hearts—forget it I ne'er can—
Before the hideous murder of that martyred man.

    *   *   *   *   *

FROM THE SPANISH

SONNET.

FROM THE SPANISH OF CERVANTES.

IF from this seething gulf and raging sea,
    Where death the wild storm threatens in each
        wave,
My life 'midst all these hard assaults I save
And reach the land again, safe, glad, and free ;
    Then, while these hands are raised on high by me,
With humble soul and mind content I'll crave
That Love may know, and Heaven itself, that gave
The sovereign good, my gratitude may see.
    My sighs then as thrice happy I shall deem
And count as pleasurable all my tears,
As cooling balm the fire that in me burns ;
    Given by Love's hand the rudest blows will seem
As help to soul and body each appears,
That to no slender good, but greatest, turns.

(See Appendix, Note A.)

13

SONNET.

FROM THE SPANISH OF GONGORA.

GOLD, no, 'tis lightning, crimson sky aglow,
    Shall best set forth the splendour of your
      morn,
Like as your purple age doth show, whose dawn
Now bears twin stars like suns upon its brow.
    Bird that is mute but emulous, although
In vain, of the more tuneful who are born
Of Art—from willow tree which leaves adorn,
Leaves that are grey, indeed, but still that grow,
    Your radiance I will sing ; how far beyond
All verse your sunrise and the hope to me
Of the bright hours with which your day will shine.
    To such great beauty let my voice respond ;
But though Apollo wills that may not be,
For yours the beauty is, the voice is mine.

(See Appendix, Note B.)

14

DECIMA.

FROM THE SPANISH OF ALARCON.

Epitaph.

BENEATH this stone a slanderer lies
  Who even spoke ill of himself;
His ashes thus laid on the shelf
This tomb doth immortalize.
He left a memory to the wise
Of living well and living ill;
With that he died against his will,
Giving all men to comprehend
How an ill deed could make an end
Of him, and all his ill words kill.

(See Appendix, Note C.)

SONETO BURLESCO.

FROM THE SPANISH OF LOPE DE VEGA.

P ROUD towers the lofty palaces between
    That once did crown those seven hills that
      rise,
And now 'gainst bare horizons to our eyes
Scarce give a sign that you have ever been !
   Ye schools of Greece, the famed abodes serene
Of Plutarchs, Platos, Xenophons—the wise :
Theatre, where wild beasts fought mid Demos' cries :
Olympiads, lustra, baths, the temple scene :
   What wondrous powers have to destruction hurled
The greatest pomp of human glory known,
With empires, arms, the wisdom of the world ?
   O solace great to my vain hope I own !
If you to such brief ruins Time has whirled,
No marvel he has spoiled my threadbare gown !

(See Appendix, Note D.)

SONETO BURLESCO.

FROM THE SPANISH OF LOPE DE VEGA.

IT was the month when most the days are fair,
   In which the flowery meads give most delight,
When first I saw you, for whom now I write,
Lady, so many foolish love-songs rare.

   Fruitless are all the pleadings that I dare ;
And, as your favour is denied me quite,
You triumph, cruel one, for in this plight
The glory is all yours, mine all the care.

   That octave verse has not turned out so ill :
But let the muses not cry fie on me
If this great sonnet ere the end I praise.

   Now I have got that sentence out ; yet still,
If, as I think, I do not end it, see,
I'll throw in a refrain of other days.

SONNET.

FROM THE SPANISH OF QUEVEDO.

THE brief year of our mortal life doth bear
    All things away, mocking the visage bold
Of valiant steel and of the marble cold
That its hard front 'gainst Time to raise would dare.
    Before the foot can walk it straight must fare
Along the way to death, whither is rolled
My life obscure; the dark sea will enfold
That poor and turbid stream in its waves drear.
    Every short moment is one long step past
Which on this march against my will I make;
At rest, asleep, I haste without reprieve.
    Then a short sigh—a bitter one—the last—
Is Death, the heritage that we must take;
But if 'tis Law, not Penalty, why grieve?

(See Appendix, Note E.)

18

DECIMA.

FROM THE SPANISH OF CALDERON.

To Lope de Vega.

ALTHOUGH the persecuting tongue
  Of envy oft the wise may fear,
No scath from it his fame shall bear,
For 'tis as though his praise it sung.
Those who most presume are stung
By envy, Lope, against thee ;
In their presumption thou wilt see
What thy glories merit : so
That those who most thy greatness show
Are those most full of jealousy.

(See Appendix, Note F.)

19

LOVE AND GLORY.

FROM THE SPANISH OF RAMON DE CAMPOAMOR.

UPON the sand and on the wind
  All things that are seem founded !
The world of earth is bounded
Like the world of the nobler mind.
Of Love and Glory aye we find
The base is naught but air and sand : ˙
Castles with which illusion's wand
The world and the heart doth fill—
Those of the world of sand are still,
Those of the heart fade in cloudland !

(See Appendix, Note G.)

20

SONNET.

FROM THE SPANISH OF LOPE DE VEGA.

OH, Christ divine ! my Life through all these
        years,
From Thy great beauty whither do I flee ?
That I affront Thy face how can it be
Which gazes on me bathed in blood and tears ?
    Filled am I with confusion and wild fears—
Knowing myself and not amending me ;
I should be shamed of so offending Thee,
My guardian angel's voice cries in my ears.
    With those pierced hands hold back my wandering
        feet,
Thou Heavenly Love ; but with what hope may I
Pray for their help who nailed them with my own ?
    O God, where have my senses been to cheat
My soul, turning my back on Thee ; and why ?
Didst Thou not on the Cross for me alone ?

FROM THE PORTUGUESE

CANTATA.

FROM THE PORTUGUESE OF GARÇÃO.

NOW in the red East afar yet faintly gleaming
    The proudly swelling sails of the swift Trojan
fleet
Amidst the azure billows of the sun-gilt ocean
Flying on the wings of the winds are hid from sight.
The wretched, hapless Dido
Doth wander through the royal palace loud lamenting,
And still with tear-swoll'n eyes in vain she seeks
    The fugitive Eneas.
Nought but deserted solitary streets and squares
The new-built Carthage to her gaze reveals :
Upon the naked shore with awful tumult breaking
Rage through the livelong night the waves in solitude :
And on the gilded pinnacles of lofty domes and
    temples
Nocturnal birds do screech with harsh foreboding
    voice.

(See Appendix, Note H.)

And from the marble sepulchre with terror she
    imagines
That from the cold ashes of the dead Sicheus
A thousand times she hears a feeble voice arise,
Crying with deep-drawn sighs, Elissa, Elissa.
Then to the awful deities of Orcus she
The sacrifices due makes ready ;
But suddenly she sees, affrighted,
Around the altars smoking with fragrant incense
A black scum boiling in the rich sculptured vessels :
    And the wine poured in libations
Seems to her eyes transformed to crimson seas of
    blood.
    She raves in wildest frenzy ;
    Pallid is grown her lovely face,
Her silken tresses flow down all dishevelled ;
Unconscious and with trembling foot she enters
The once delightful chamber
Where from the now faithless lover
    She heard with deep emotion
Sighs so heartbroken mingled with soft complaints.
But there the cruel Fates did show to her
The Ilian garments, that still hanging
From the gilded couch with dazzling gleam re-
    vealed
The glittering shield and the bright Teucrian sword.

With a convulsive hand she snatches suddenly
From out its sheath the blade refulgent,
And on the adamantine piercing steel
Her tender breast snow-white and crystalline she
    hurls :
And in bubbles of foam plashing and murmuring
Leaps the hot life-blood forth from the deadly wound :
With the red-spouting gore bedewed and sprinkled
Tremble the Doric columns of the hall.
Thrice does she strive in vain to rise,
And three times fainting back upon the couch again
Her body falls, while unto Heaven she raises
Her tortured dying eyes.
Then gazing at the lustrous armour
Of the fled Dardan chief,
These her last utterances did she repeat,
And the most pitiful and mournful accents
Still floating through the golden arches of the roof
Long afterwards were heard in plaintive sad lament.

    O ye sweet treasures
    Source of deep pleasures
    To my glad eyne,
    While Fate beguiled
    And the Gods smiled
    Consent benign :

Of Dido mournful
The soul receive,
From all these troubles
My heart relieve.
Unhappy Dido
Has lived out her days :
She of proud Carthage
The high walls did raise.
Now naked and bare
Her shade alone
In Charon's bark there,
The hideous one,
Goes ploughing the stream
Black as night without gleam
Of Phlegethon.

SONNET.

FROM THE PORTUGUESE OF CAMOENS.

L OVE is a fire whose flame doth burn unseen
   A wound whose aching smart we do not fee
Contentment discontent with its own weal ;
A teasing pain, though neither deep nor keen :
  It is *not* liking more than liking e'en ;
Wandering alone 'midst crowds that seem unreal ;
Not to content one's self with Heaven's own seal ;
A care that only gain by loss doth mean :
  'Tis to be captured with one's own consent ;
The victor to the vanquished here must serve ;
Keep faith with one who on our death is bent :
  How can its fickle favour e'er preserve
In human hearts consistence of intent,
Since to itself contrarious Love doth swerve?

SONNET.

FROM THE PORTUGUESE OF CAMOENS.

A S shepherd Jacob served seven weary years
    Laban for Rachel, fairest mountaineer,
But not the father did he serve, 'twas her;
For her alone as his reward he cares.

  His days in hope of one sole day he bears,
Himself with sight of her contenting there;
But using guile her father, trickster rare,
Instead of Rachel's hand now gave him Leah's.

  The shepherd sad, seeing that with deceit
His shepherdess was thus to him denied,
As were he undeserving of his wife,

  Began to serve seven other years complete,
Saying: More would I gladly serve beside
Were not, for love so long, so short our life.

THE SONG OF THE EXILE.

FROM THE PORTUGUESE OF GONÇALVES DIAS.

MINE is the land where waves the palm
    And where the tuneful thrush doth sing :
The birds that here make minstrelsy
    Have harsher note and duller wing.

Our sky has more and brighter stars,
    Our fields are full of dazzling flowers,
Our forests glow with richer life,
    More love breathes through our life's glad hours.

And when at night alone I muse
    I find a deeper pleasure there,
In my own glorious land of palms,
    Where the birds' music fills the air.

(See Appendix, Note I.)

My country has such varied charms,
 I ne'er can find aught like them here ;
And when alone at night I muse
 I find a deeper pleasure there :
Mine is the glorious land of palms,
 Where the thrush pours its music rare.

God grant me that I may not die
 Until I home return again,
Once more to gaze on beauties there
 Which here I ever seek in vain :
Until again I see the palms
 And hear the thrush's flute-like strain.

THE SONG OF THE TAMOYO.*

FROM THE PORTUGUESE OF GONÇALVES DIAS.

WEEP thou not, little son,
   Oh, weep not, for life
Is a desperate strife ;
   'Tis a fight hard and long.
If the combat unsparing
Make the weak cower despairing,
It can but inspirit
   The brave and the strong.

We live but a day long !
The strong fears not dying,
'Tis the thought of base flying
   Alone he can fear ;
And swift his bow bending,
His shaft surely sending,
He strikes down a foeman,
   Condor or tapir.†

* The Tamoyos were the tribe of Indians who originally inhabited the province of Rio de Janeiro in Brazil.
† Tapir is pronounced *tapeer*.

The strong man, the craven,
Alike envy his daring,
When they see him, uncaring,
  In the battle rejoice ;
And their hoary heads bending,
The old men attending,
In solemn war councils,
  Shall list to his voice.

If thou livest, be chief,
If thou die well thou'lt sleep,
And thy tribe still shall keep
  Thy fame bright and clear ;
For thy life never caring,
Be brave and be strong !
Till death 'tis not long,
  Then of death have no fear.

Since thy forefathers fought,
Let their spirit adorn thee ;
A Tamoyo has borne thee,
  Thou shalt prove thy valour.
Be a warrior peerless,
Strong, hardy and fearless,
The pride of thy people
  In peace and in war.

36

But if traitorous fortune,
In some direful hour,
Hurl thee into the power
    Of the treacherous foe ;
When the last moment's near
Be thou calm, without fear,
Remember thy bold deeds,
    The warrior dies so !

And fall like some great tree
When riven asunder
Down crashes like thunder
    Its vast length on the ground ;
So the strong man should die !
As life fades from his eye
He triumphs, his glory
Shall wider resound.

Then try thou thine arms,
Into life hew thy way,
Whether gloomy or gay
    'Tis a fight hard and long ;
If the combat unsparing
Make the weak cower despairing,
It can but inspirit
    The brave and the strong.

A RHAPSODY.

FROM THE PORTUGUESE OF GONÇALVES DIAS.

A H ! let me not die without finding at least
    For a moment, it may be, in life's weary waste
A love that is equal to mine :
Grant, Heavenly Powers, that on earth I may meet
An angel, a woman, your handiwork sweet,
    Whose feelings with mine may entwine.

A soul that is sister to mine, and whose eyes
Can read my heart's thought though unuttered, and
    rise
    Through joy's broad clear sunshine with me ;
Then united, bound close, with a tie none may sever,
To the heavens we will soar, leaving earth's gloom
    for ever,
    Rapt in love's endless ecstasy.

FROM THE ITALIAN

SONNET.

FROM THE ITALIAN OF PETRARCH.

I FELT already in my heart grow less
   The spirit that from you receives its life ;
And since each earthly creature in its strife
'Gainst death doth naturally seek redress,

   I loosed Desire, now curbed with much duress,
And sent it on the almost forgotten way
Whither, indeed, it calls me night and day,
But I lead elsewhere its unwillingness.

   Me shamefaced and lingering did it bring
To see again those sweet eyes, which I fly
For fear that I to them be wearying.

   Now I shall live awhile ; for there doth lie
In but your glance such power o'er my life's spring ;
Then, if I yield not to Desire, I die.

(See Appendix, Note J.)

CHORUS

WHAT Death would loosen thou, O Love, dost
    bind,
The friend of Peace art thou, as he of War,
And in her triumph dost triumphant reign :
When round two gentle souls thy fetters wind
Thou makest Earth seem as the Heavens are,
While yet to dwell here thou dost not disdain.
On high there is no anger : men regain
From thee tranquillity : and inward hate,
Seignior, thou drivest from each gracious heart :
A thousand Furies at thy glance depart :
Thy force supernal can almost create
From mortal things one glad eternal state.

FROM THE SWEDISH

THE BRAZILIAN MAID.

FROM THE SWEDISH OF COUNT SNOILSKY.

I.

NO, I shall ne'er forget the wondrous girl
　　Who shone at the Seine Prefect's fête so
bright ;
Star of Brazil—a stray guest of the night
'Midst Europe's puppets deep in fashion's whirl.
Fresh as South-West wind o'er Atlantic swirl,
She calmly gazed around with great clear eyes :
Each painted belle felt danger's keen surmise,
Fluttered each heart in cage of silk and pearl.
To stately *grand-croix* scarce a glance she threw,
Daughter of ancient forests, in whose sky
Glitters the Southern Cross the dusk night through.
We all drew near with words of flattery.
Then smiled America at Europe's crew
With laugh unmoved that rang most silvery.

(See Appendix, Note K.)

45

Once did I listen to a traveller old —
A seaman, weather-beaten, rough, was he —
Telling his tale of wanderings bold and free
Through tropic forests which new worlds enfold ;
A network grown for ages, uncontrolled,
Of climbing plants which no steel may sever,
Where nature's barrier mocks man's endeavour,
Blunting his axe's edge and crying ' Hold !'
Then, so 'tis said, resounds through leafy night
A laugh defiant, of unmeasured scorn
And challenge to the Old World's unequal might.
That wondrous voice is of the forest born,
And Pan through it of cultured man makes light.
Fair maid, learn'dst thou that laugh from sylvan faun ?

VELAZQUEZ.*

FROM THE SWEDISH OF COUNT SNOILSKY.

THE Beautiful in Art is but the True?
　　Then stands Velazquez, laurel - crowned
　　　alone :
Each stroke he draws seems life and force to own,
Limns he a princeling or a beggar crew.
Each pikeman's face looks out with swarthy hue,
As if well known, from misty Flemish days,
When Breda's governor gives the city keys
To brave Spinola—pledge of victory due.
Look at ' The Topers !' blissful, rosy red,
They reck not of their shirtless, sorry plight,
While down the ivy-wreath slips round the head.
So paints Velazquez and one other wight :
Poet, ' of brow with melancholy spread,'
Come not, I pray, with Raphael's name forthright.

* The principal works of the great Spanish painter, Velazquez,
are in the Museo in Madrid. The masterpieces referred to in
the sonnet are named respectively ' Las Lanzas ' (the surrender
of Breda) and ' Los Borrachos.'

THOROUGH.

FROM THE SWEDISH OF COUNT SNOILSKY.

ONE and one only must thy purpose be,
    Whole and decided :
From giant force but pygmy deed wouldst see
    Were it divided.

Thou must at once thy choice for ever make,
    For strife or pleasure :
Must choose the kernel or the husk to take—
    Repent at leisure.

Some seek for pearls, others for bubbles mere,
    On life's sea cruising :
Complain not if the bubble disappear—
    'Twas thine own choosing.

FROM THE GERMAN

D

TO PETRARCH.

FROM THE GERMAN OF UHLAND.

IF truth of Laura thou hast sung indeed,
   Her saintly look, and gracious, heavenly mien—
And far from me be doubt or question keen
Of that which was thy soul's most inward creed !
Was she a flower sprung from celestial seed—
   An angel amidst toil and strife terrene—
   A gentle stranger on this earth's rough scene
That homeward soon her winged flight did speed ?
Then do I fear that on yon golden star
   Where thou, transfigured, now at last art come,
     Thou never wilt the longed-for one regain ;
For she has flown meanwhile on high afar,
   In holier spheres received has found her home,
     And thou must sing thy love lament again.

THE FOREST WITCH.*

FROM THE GERMAN OF G. VON BODDIEN.

A HORSEMAN rides at wildest speed through
    wood, o'er brier and bracken,
Nor will he heed the hovering form that becks his
    course to slacken ;
' My couch is not on sunny heath, nor in the forest
    gloaming,
Afar from me my bright love waits, and Cease, she
    cries, thy roaming.

' Begone, begone, thou phantom shape, why dost
    thou vainly follow ?
Too cold thy slender cloudy form, thine eyes are dead
    and hollow !
My love has whiter arms than thou, her eyes like stars
    are gleaming,
Her kiss is warm, her laugh rings clear, thy threaten-
    ing is but seeming.'

* Written for Rubinstein's music. Published by Stanley
Lucas, Weber and Co., New Bond Street.

52

The heron screams, the charger's flanks 'neath bloody
    spurs are streaming,
The woman's form towers giant high ! Is this awake
    or dreaming ?
On, on they fly through wood, o'er wold, till like a
    vulture stooping
With clutch and dash the shape descends, upon the
    bridle swooping ;

And now she has him by the arm, while through the
    darkness crashing,
The air grows hot, the rider swoons, the witch's eyes
    are flashing.
Two paces from the fallen steed there in the forest
    gloaming
The horseman in her arms lies dead, and 'Cease,'
    love cries, ' thy roaming !'

PHILOSOPHY OF HISTORY

FROM THE GERMAN OF PAUL HEYSE.

WIDER the world's delights are teeming,
    More deep or high they hardly seem,
Though more good folks to-day are dreaming
In pleasant guise this life's old dream.
Yet he whose day began among
The group on Plato's lips that hung,
Who saw in Phidias' studio
A godlike form from marble grow,
Heard in the theatre at even
Antigone with Greek chorus given,
And with Aspasia and her coterie
Might sup as a familiar votary,
Has writ more pleasure on life's pages
Than we have after all these ages.

FROM THE DUTCH

SONNET.

FROM THE DUTCH OF PIETER CORNELISZOON HOOFT.

HOPE'S guiding stars, ye planets of my youth,
　　Eyes that I know are lit from heaven's fire,
You, when your windows close, from me retire
My life's support, joys full of tender truth ;
For you shut in a gladdening power, in sooth,
And friendly gaiety : Love with all its quire,
Wit, laughter, and each grace therein conspire,
And a whole world of charm and pleasure both.
Nature, who seems entombed in mists that lower,
Wanting your brightness, mourns her richest dower,
That you enshrine in space so narrow made ;
Yet 'tis not narrow, as without it seems,
But wide and wild enough to hold all dreams,
Wherein my fickle soul so far has strayed.

(See Appendix, Note L.)

SONNET.

FROM THE DUTCH OF PIETER CORNELISZOON HOOFT.

M Y Lady, Love, and I—hard strife have we,
    Wherein all three may well be overthrown,
For I and Love aye burn for her alone,
And she loves but herself, spite Love and me.
If she through her self-love her ruin see,
Love without her will not long make his moan ;
And if you die, O Love, I too must own
My life, whose stay you were, will ended be.
Yet if it so befall not, what wait I
But grief from pain ?   Lament from misery?
Woe from my smart ?   Despair from all my fear ?
Whilst Love himself my Lady comes to woo,
Who loves herself: when were foes like these two
In all the world so hard to lover e'er ?

APPENDIX

WITH the exception of Cervantes and Calderon, probably very few of the Spanish poets of the sixteenth and seventeenth centuries are well known in this country ; and Camoens is almost the only Portuguese poet whose name is familiar to English ears. It may, therefore, not be out of place to add one or two brief notes on some of those writers from whom translations are given.

Note A.

Page 13.—CERVANTES (1547-1616) is best known to us by his *Don Quixote*, but he wrote many plays, some of which remain, and various tales, as well as pastoral romances. The sonnet is from one of the latter, entitled *Galatea.*

Note B.

Page 14.—It was GONGORA (1561-1627) who first introduced the 'cultivated style' into Spanish literature. The poems written by him in his earlier period possess a certain simplicity and dignity, but as these did not succeed in attracting attention, he adopted the affected and extravagant manner, which had many imitators and is classed as 'Gongorism.' He is too often unintelligible to the best critics among his countrymen, and commentaries have been written to elucidate his obscure meaning.

NOTE C.

Page 15.—JUAN RUIZ DE ALARCON Y MENDOZA born in Mexico ; died in Spain, 1639) may be classed with the most eminent Spanish dramatists of that brilliant period of the National Theatre. This Decima ' (ten-line stanza) was written by him on a nobleman of unamiable reputation.

NOTE D.

Page 16.—The real founder of the Spanish theatre was LOPE DE VEGA (1562-1635). The fertility of his genius is astounding ; he is said to have written 1,500 plays, and these, with the epics, pastorals, odes, and sonnets, which he continually poured forth, gained for him the foremost place among his contemporaries. He took priest's orders about 1614.

NOTE E.

Page 18.—QUEVEDO (1570-1647) attained his celebrity principally as a prose writer, by his theological and metaphysical works, and also by his satires. Naturally, however, his striking compositions in verse are more popular, and from these the sonnet is taken.

Note F.

Page 19.—With great powers of imagination and invention, CALDERON (1600-1681) yet takes rank below his master, Lope de Vega. Some two hundred plays and *autos* were written by him, and with Philip IV. as his patron he furnished numerous dramatic spectacles for the Court.

Note G.

Page 20.—This 'Decima' is from the *Doloras* of the eminent living Spanish poet CAMPOAMOR.

Note H.

Page 27.—The *Cantata de Dido* is introduced in a scene of the comedy entitled *Assembléa ou Partida*, by PEDRO ANTONIO CORREA GARÇÃO (1724-1772). A splendid *edition de luxe* of his works (sonnets, odes, satires, epistles, and dramatic pieces) has been published by the distinguished Brazilian delegate in London, the Conselheiro J. A. de Azevedo Castro, who has thus rendered a great literary service to Portugal.

Note I.

Page 33.—ANTONIO GONÇALVES DIAS (1823-1864) is regarded as the great representative poet of Brazil. The *Canção do Exilio*, written by him while at the University of Coimbra, in Portugal, is probably the best known of his compositions. He was a journalist, a dramatist, and a Government official ; he visited Europe three times, and died on his last voyage home to Rio de Janeiro.

Note J.

Page 41.—Sonetto XXXIX. (in the *Canzoniere*, 32), *In Vita di Madonna Laura.*

Note K.

Page 45.—The poems translated from the Swedish are from an early volume of Count SNOILSKY (who continues to write), published in Stockholm and entitled *Dikter.*

Note L.

Page 57.—HOOFT (1581-1647) is one of the most distinguished poets of the Republic of the Netherlands. Besides his lesser productions he wrote several tragedies, and may be considered the founder of the Dutch stage. He achieved equal celebrity in prose, his *History of the Netherlands* being a model of style.